One-Minute Challenges

English

by Linda Aber

Watermill Press

For Corey Mackenzie Aber and Kip Alexander Aber

This edition published in 2002.

Printed in Canada

10 9 8 7 6 5 4

INTRODUCTION

Take the One-Minute English Challenge . . . IF You Dare!

What you don't know won't hurt you. But what you do know will definitely help you beat the clock in this brain-straining, giggle-gaining book of *One-Minute Challenges*.

Sharpen your pencils, then sharpen your wits with timed pun-filled punctuation puzzles, word searches, grammar skill builders, spelling bees, magic word squares, and just-for-fun wordplay games. Test yourself, test your friends, then test the best of the rest. You'll be amazed at how quickly you master each group of English challenges.

Select the challenge of your choice. Read the instructions before you start the timer. Use an egg timer or a watch with a second hand to time yourself. See how much you can finish in one minute. Check your work, then check the timer. Did you finish early? If you did, go for the Bonus Round and pick up some extra practice. Beat the clock, then go back and beat your own record!

All the answers are in the back of the book, but don't peek until you're really sure you don't have the answer stuck somewhere in that magnificent brain of yours!

Are you ready to beat the clock and the book? On your mark. Get set. Go!—to the first test, that is!

Challenge #1

Hooray for Homonyms!

A homonym is a word that sounds the same as another word or words but has a different meaning and is spelled differently. Read the sentence, then circle the correct homonym to fit the definition. How many can you correctly circle in one minute?

1. Is it rude to STAIR or STARE?
2. Is a teddy a BARE or BEAR?
3. Is a buzzing insect a BEE or BE?
4. Do you sail out to SEE or SEA?
5. If you've gotten bigger, have you GROWN or GROAN?
6. Is money borrowed a LONE or a LOAN?
7. Does blood go through a VANE, VEIN, or VAIN?
8. Is the horse's hair a MAINE, MANE, or MAIN?
9. Are seven days a WEAK or WEEK?
10. Will you climb to a mountain's PEEK or PEAK?
11. Do you eat a STAKE or STEAK?
12. Will a window BRAKE or BREAK?
13. Is the glass a PAIN or PANE?
14. Does the king REIN, REIGN, or RAIN?
15. Do clocks strike on the OUR or HOUR?
16. Is bread made with FLOUR or FLOWER?
17. If you change the color, do you DYE or DIE?
18. If you are near are you BUY or BY?

19. Is money owed DEW or DUE?

20. Is a female sheep a YOU or EWE?

21. Is clothing what you WARE or WEAR?

22. Do bald men lack HARE or HAIR?

23. Is to carry to HALL or HAUL?

24. Is to cry to BALL or BAWL?

25. Does a chimney have a FLUE or FLEW?

26. Is also TWO, TO, or TOO?

27. Is a man in armor a NIGHT or KNIGHT?

28. Is a letter what you RIGHT or WRITE?

29. When the game is over have you ONE or WON?

30. Is the greatest star the SUN or SON?

31. When your voice is scratchy are you HORSE or HOARSE?

32. When something's rough is it COURSE or COARSE?

33. When you listen do you HEAR or HERE?

34. Does the boat dock at the PIER or PEER?

35. Is all of something HOLE or WHOLE?

36. Is a part in a play a ROLL or ROLE?

37. Do you breathe the HEIR or AIR?

38. Do you eat a PAIR, PARE, or PEAR?

39. Is a bucket a PALE or PAIL?

40. Will the boat have a SALE or SAIL?

BONUS ROUND!

If you finished in less than a minute, try these bonus questions for extra points!

41. Popcorn has a COLONEL or KERNEL?

42. Is a youngster a MINOR or MINER?

CHALLENGE #2

CONTRACTION DISTRACTION!

A contraction is one word made from two words by leaving out one or more letters and replacing them with an apostrophe ('). See how many contractions you can correctly make in one minute.

1. let us _____

2. he is _____

3. they have _____

4. were not _____

5. here is _____

6. she is _____

7. they are _____

8. what is _____

9. has not _____

10. we will _____

11. that is _____

12. do not _____

13. cannot _____

14. I would _____

15. they will _____

16. you will _____

17. I have _____

18. it is _____

19. you are _____

20. did not _____

21. she will _____

22. you have _____

23. are not _____

24. there is _____

25. I will _____

26. is not _____

27. who is _____

28. will not _____

29. was not _____

30. she would _____

31. does not _____

32. he will _____

BONUS ROUND!

If you finished in less than a minute, try these bonus questions for extra points! Change the contraction back into two words.

33. haven't _____

34. you'll _____

35. we've _____

36. couldn't _____

37. they'd _____

38. shouldn't _____

Challenge #3

Exciting, Incredible, Fabulous Adjective Word Search

An adjective is a word that describes something or somebody. Using the list of adjectives here, how many can you find and circle in one minute? Look for adjectives going up, down, backward, forward, and diagonally.

Adjective List:

hot	blue	slippery	tired	dirty
greasy	crisp	rough	baked	big
old	many	early	funny	bitter
noisy	fat	long	ten	bad
wet	used	dim	scared	red
soft	white	sad	top	ripe
sweet	fast			

```
S W E E T E T I H W Y
G L O N G I B X Z B S
R T I R E D E K A B I
E M E P I R E D J I O
A A I R P S I R C T N
S N T D F E U L B T Y
Y Y F O E A R L Y E N
S P O T H N T Y X R N
A L S C A R E D E S U
D R O U G H W T S A F
```

7

CHALLENGE #4

RHYME TIME

Are you a poet but you don't know it? Here's your chance to show it! Set the timer for one minute. Then see how many words rhyming with the word *GREAT* you can write down before your time is up.

GREAT

1. _____	2. _____	3. _____	4. _____
5. _____	6. _____	7. _____	8. _____
9. _____	10. _____	11. _____	12. _____
13. _____	14. _____	15. _____	16. _____
17. _____	18. _____	19. _____	20. _____
21. _____	22. _____	23. _____	24. _____
25. _____	26. _____	27. _____	28. _____
29. _____	30. _____		

BONUS ROUND!

If you thought of 30 words in less than a minute, your bonus round is this: TAKE A WELL-DESERVED REST!

Or, quickly, in the time you have left write down ten words that rhyme with the word REST.

1. _____	2. _____	3. _____	4. _____
5. _____	6. _____	7. _____	8. _____
9. _____	10. _____		

CHALLENGE #5

SHHHH! SILENT LETTER ZONE!

There are 26 letters in the alphabet. For as many letters of the alphabet as possible, try to find a word in which that letter is silent. See how many you can write down in one minute. (Example: in Zone, the *e* is silent.)

A _____ B _____ C _____

D _____ E _____ F _____

G _____ H _____ I _____

J _____ K _____ L _____

M _____ N _____ O _____

P _____ Q _____ R _____

S _____ T _____ U _____

V _____ W _____ X _____

Y _____ Z _____

CHALLENGE #6

PALINDROME CROSSWORD

A palindrome is a word, phrase, verse, or sentence that reads the same way backward as it does forward. The answers in this crossword puzzle are all one-word palindromes (except for one tricky answer). Use the clues to help you. Give yourself a minute and see how much of the puzzle you can complete. (If time runs out, finish it just for fun.)

Across
1. Slang for mother.
3. A formal way to address a woman.
5. A firecracker that won't pop.
6. Slang for statistics.
8. Songs sung alone.
10. You see with it.

Down
2. To be silent.
4. Slang for father.
5. A bird that is extinct.
7. Slang for a girl sibling.
9. Even, flat.
11. The night before Christmas.

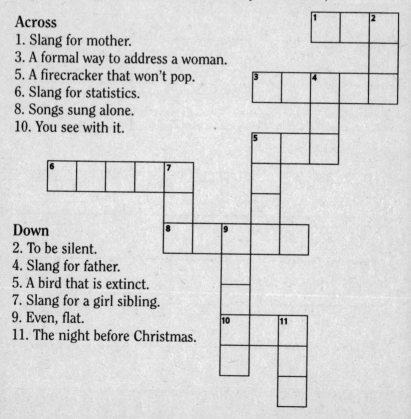

10

CHALLENGE #7

EI, IE, OH NO!

You know the old *i* before *e* rule, right? "Put *i* before *e* except after *c*, or when sounded like *a* as in *neighbor* and *weigh*." Sound easy? Fill in the blanks with either *ie* or *ei* to complete the words correctly. How many can you do in one minute? (*Hint*: It may be helpful to say the words out loud. If there is a word you don't know, go on the next one. Remember, every second counts!)

1. n____ther
2. gr____ve
3. v____w
4. br____f
5. ch____f
6. h____ght
7. fr____nd
8. bel____ve
9. conc____t
10. b____ge
11. rel____f
12. c____ling
13. misch____f
14. p____ce
15. s____ze
16. forf____t
17. prot____n

18. anc____nt
19. sl____ght
20. dec____ve
21. rec____pt
22. sh____ld
23. caff____ne
24. pr____st
25. th____f
26. r____gn
27. f____ld
28. hyg____ne
29. s____ge
30. sover____gn
31. glac____r
32. sc____nce
33. spec____s
34. h____r

35. r____ndeer
36. w____ght
37. n____ghbor
38. cash____r
39. consc____nce
40. gr____f
41. bes____ge
42. s____ve
43. w____rd
44. bel____f
45. p____rce
46. shr____k
47. front____r
48. effic____nt
49. counterf____t
50. ach____ve

11

WORD REBUS RIDDLES

These word pictures are called rebuses. Each rebus is a riddle. Your job is to see how many rebus riddles you can solve in a minute. Study each word rebus and try to figure out what the word picture stands for.

An example is: $\dfrac{\text{MAN}}{\text{BOARD}}$ = MAN OVERBOARD

1.
```
      R
      O
R  O  A  D  S
      D
      S
```
_____

2. GROUND
    FEET
    FEET
    FEET
    FEET
    FEET
    FEET
_____

3.
```
      T
      O
      U
      C
      H
```
_____

4. ‥‥‥‥‥SIGN‥‥‥‥‥
_____

5.
```
ME
AL
```
_____

6. ONE   ANOTHER
    ONE   ANOTHER
    ONE   ANOTHER
    ONE   ANOTHER
    ONE   ANOTHER
    ONE   ANOTHER
_____

7. ONAHOLEE
_____

8.
```
        N  T  A
     O  U        I
     MOLEHILL    N
```
_____

9.
```
        N
KEY  W ←↕→ E
        S
```
_____

12

CHALLENGE #9

STATE ABBREVIATIONS

Through wind, rain, sleet, or snow, the mail must go through! To help the mail go through faster, the postal service requires two-letter abbreviations for the states. How many of the 50 states can you correctly abbreviate in one minute?

____Alabama	____Louisiana	____Ohio
____Alaska	____Maine	____Oklahoma
____Arizona	____Maryland	____Oregon
____Arkansas	____Massachusetts	____Pennsylvania
____California	____Michigan	____Rhode Island
____Colorado	____Minnesota	____South Carolina
____Connecticut	____Mississippi	____South Dakota
____Delaware	____Missouri	____Tennessee
____Florida	____Montana	____Texas
____Georgia	____Nebraska	____Utah
____Hawaii	____Nevada	____Vermont
____Idaho	____New Hampshire	____Virginia
____Illinois	____New Jersey	____Washington
____Indiana	____New Mexico	____West Virginia
____Iowa	____New York	____Wisconsin
____Kansas	____North Carolina	____Wyoming
____Kentucky	____North Dakota	

BONUS ROUND!

If you finished in less than a minute, try abbreviating these territories and districts.

____Canal Zone	____District of Columbia	____Guam
____Puerto Rico	____Virgin Islands	

Challenge #10

A Capital Offense!

Read the story once before you set the timer. Then, set the timer for one minute and circle each letter you find that needs capitalizing. When one minute is up, count the circles you've made. Remember to look for first words in a sentence, names of people and places, the pronoun I, and words of family relationships when used as a person's name.

the thing in the lake

on saturday, july 14, mom, dad, and i drove to sebago lake. i was hoping the morris family and their big bully of a son, butch, wouldn't be there waiting for us. well, butch was there all right, but so was something else. everybody was talking about the monster in the lake.

"sheriff johnson and his deputy stayed up all night watching for it," said butch's aunt harriet. "they're calling the thing nessie, after the loch ness monster. if you ask me, i think it's just a big old carp."

"no child of mine is going to be bait for a lake monster," mom told dad. "i think we should get in the car and go back home to our house on pine street in our safe little town of pine bluffs, massachusetts. the only monsters there are the dust balls under the bed!"

just as i was about to complain, i turned for one last look at sebago lake. guess what i saw waving at me from out in the middle of the lake? butch morris, who else. it was all his idea of one big joke. the laugh was on him, though, because right behind him something else was waving, too. it was nessie, the thing in the lake! when butch saw the monster behind him, he swam ashore as fast as he could.

butch and his family left and never came back to the lake. as for mom, dad, and me, we stayed and had the best summer ever. butch's aunt was right. the "monster" was just a big fish. it's in an aquarium in boston now. thanks to the monster, the really scary thing in the lake is gone! bye, butch. i don't miss you at all!

CHALLENGE #11

TWO WORDS = ONE

Compound words are two words combined to make one. Draw a line from the sets of five words in Column A to the five words in Column B to make as many sets of compound words as you can in one minute.

	Column A	Column B
1.	arm	worm
	down	person
	bare	chair
	earth	pour
	chair	back
2.	tear	tag
	birth	bird
	name	wide
	black	drop
	world	place
3.	score	paper
	knap	wreck
	knock	card
	news	out
	ship	sack
4.	text	case
	broom	light
	flag	stick
	suit	book
	moon	pole
5.	team	born
	street	mate
	new	car
	chalk	work
	play	board

CHALLENGE #12

SCRAMBLED WORDS

Unscramble the three letters on the left and write a new word in the space on the right. How many new words can you make in a minute? yTr ti! (That's "Try it!")

how _____	tra _____	yna _____
atc _____	oer _____	dha _____
xob _____	rac _____	ent _____
dna _____	tib _____	ubn _____
pil _____	dlo _____	tho _____
rae _____	tha _____	oto _____
upt _____	atp _____	woh _____
usb _____	gub _____	fde _____
mmo _____	ubt _____	gdi _____
wot _____	pag _____	eeb _____
unt _____	rof _____	anp _____
kao _____	arf _____	yee _____
eon _____	ufn _____	rao _____
pho _____	nug _____	ozo _____
wes _____	eus _____	pam _____
nam _____	hes _____	dba _____

BONUS ROUND!

If you finished them all in less than a minute, try these four-letter words for extra fun.

ndah _____   adeh _____

raih _____   lpeh _____

16

Challenge #13

Word in a Word

Each capitalized word has another word hidden in it. The clues will help you find the hidden words. Underline them. How many can you find in one minute?

Find a winged thing in BEAT,
And an auto in CARE.
Something warm is in WHEAT,
A long distance in FAIR.
There's a bug tucked in PANT,
And a boy's name in BEAN.
Find a plot in a PLANT,
And a number in TEEN.
There's a nap in CREST,
And a tool in SHOE.
A direction's in WREST.
More than one is in FLEW.
Find a fruit in APPEAR,
And a listener in HEAR.
There's a buddy in PAIL,
And a good buy in SCALE.
Something legal's in CLAW,
Something uncooked in DRAW.
There's a question in CHOW,
Something not high in PLOW.
Two times five is in TREND,
And the last line's in SEND.

17

CHALLENGE #14

LET'S COMPARE PAIRS

An analogy is a comparison between two pairs of items. The first pair of items is related in the same way as the second pair. For example:

HARD is to ROCK as SOFT is to COTTON.

Use the words in the word bank to finish each analogy. Set the timer for one minute and complete as many as you can.

Word Bank

floor	hat	taste	water	vegetable
empty	ship	down	enclosing	painting
sled	eleventh	swimming	thermometer	glove

1. BLOUSE is to SHIRT as BONNET is to _____.
2. WRITER is to BOOK as ARTIST is to _____.
3. BIRD is to FLYING as FISH is to _____.
4. WALLPAPER is to WALL as RUG is to _____.
5. TRUTH is to LIE as FULL is to _____.
6. APPLE is to FRUIT as CORN is to _____.
7. NOSE is to SMELL as TONGUE is to _____.
8. KNIFE is to CUTTING as FENCE is to _____.
9. CAR is to LAND as BOAT is to _____.
10. ASTRONAUT is to SPACESHIP as SAILOR is to _____.
11. HEAD is to HELMET as HAND is to _____.
12. NONSENSE is to SENSE as UP is to _____.
13. SECOND is to THIRD as TENTH is to _____.
14. HORSE is to CARRIAGE as DOG is to _____.
15. TIME is to CLOCK as TEMPERATURE is to _____.

CHALLENGE #15

HOMONYM CROSSWORD

All of the answers in this crossword puzzle are homonyms, words that sound the same but are spelled differently from the clues below and have different meanings. Set your timer for one minute and try to beat the clock!

Across
3. GROWN
4. WEIGHT
6. BEE
7. MEET
9. ORE and OR
10. DO or DEW

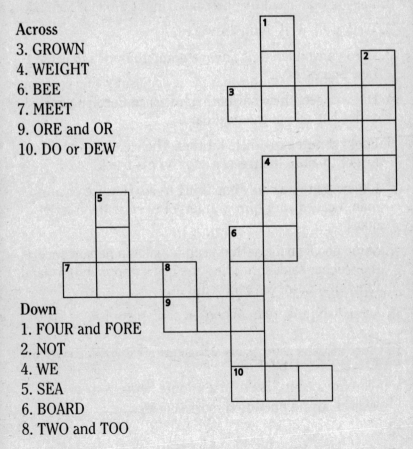

Down
1. FOUR and FORE
2. NOT
4. WE
5. SEA
6. BOARD
8. TWO and TOO

19

CHALLENGE #16

NOTABLE QUOTES

Of course you know quotation marks are used to enclose a speaker's exact words. Using that rule, take one minute to correctly place quotation marks in the following sentences.

1. Did you hear about the three holes in the ground? Sam asked.

2. Well, well, well, John answered.

3. Carolyn wondered, Is anyone going to notice that I got new braces?

4. Did you get a new haircut? John asked Carolyn when she arrived at school the next day.

5. Look! shouted my little brother. The ice cream man forgot to close the freezer door on his truck!

6. I knew there was only one thing to do. Hey, ice cream man, I called after him, you forgot to close the freezer door!

7. Some people believe that pepper makes a person sneeze, the teacher said, sprinkling the black grains in her hand. I myself have never believed that.

8. Achoo! she sneezed. Achoo! Achoo! Achoo!

BONUS ROUND!

If you finished in less than a minute, write your own sentence, using quotation marks correctly.

CHALLENGE #17

ALPHABET SOUP

What's your initial response to this first initials test? Each set of initials equals what the number stands for. The first one has been done for you. How many of the rest can you guess in a minute?

1. 26 = L of the A   <u>Letters of the Alphabet</u>

2. 4 and 20 = B B in a P   _____

3. 9 = P in the S S   _____

4. 24 = H in a D   _____

5. 12 = M in the Y   _____

6. 7 = D in a W   _____

7. 4 = Q in a G   _____

8. 13 = S on the U.S. F   _____

9. 52 (53) = C in a D (with the J) _____

10. 90 = D in a R A   _____

11. 11 = P on a F T   _____

12. 3 = B M "S H T R"   _____

CHALLENGE #18

SIMILES

A simile is a figure of speech that compares one thing to another using the word "like" or "as." The similes here have been split up. Draw a line from Column A to Column B to match the first part of a simile to the word that correctly finishes it. How many can you complete in one minute?

Column A	Column B
Blind as a	pancake.
Dead as a	bug in a rug.
Cold as	fruitcake.
Flat as a	tack.
Quiet as a	peacock.
Snug as a	pig.
Old as the	doornail.
Sly as a	ice.
Neat as a	bee.
Light as a	molasses.
Fit as a	fox.
Busy as a	mouse.
Slow as	pin.
Fat as a	bat.
Proud as a	hills.
Nutty as a	feather.
Sharp as a	fiddle.

CHALLENGE #19

WHAT'S UNUSUAL ABOUT THIS PARAGRAPH?

In the paragraph below there is something quite unusual. Set the timer for one minute. Read the paragraph over and over and see if you can solve this mystery before your time is up.

A Most Unusual Paragraph

What is so unusual about this paragraph? You won't find too many paragraphs similar to it. Look at it and study it. You may not find out what is out of the ordinary right away. Study it again. At first you may fail in your task. But if you stay with it long you will find the solution. Think. What is odd about it? Look and look again. Do you want a hint? Sorry. No hints for you today or tomorrow. You must do this without asking for hints. It's a most unusual paragraph, would you not say so? But why? That's what you must find out now. Good luck!

Write your answer here:

_____

CHALLENGE #20

TO -GE OR NOT TO -DGE?
THAT IS THE QUESTION!

At the end of a word, the "j" sound can be spelled -ge or -dge.
-Dge is used at the end of a word or syllable directly after a single
short vowel. -Ge is used after a consonant, after a long vowel
sound, and after two vowels. Those are the rules to follow as you
see how many of the words here are spelled correctly. Write T for
True if a word is spelled right, and F for False if it's spelled wrong.
Ready? Set the timer for one minute, then begin!

1.____brige   12.____bage   23.____range
2.____age   13.____huge   24.____smudge
3.____juge   14.____radge   25.____stage
4.____porrige   15.____arrange   26.____urdge
5.____hinge   16.____verdge   27.____dredge
6.____knowlege   17.____merdge   28.____fuge
7.____strange   18.____truge   29.____doge
8.____goudge   19.____sponge   30.____cartrige
9.____fordge   20.____page   31.____change
10.____rige   21.____couradge   32.____lardge
11.____cadge   22.____plege   33.____partrige

BONUS ROUND!

If you finished this in less than a minute, try these for
extra fun: 34. ____anchoradge 35. ____Dodgers

CHALLENGE #21

SLING THE SLANG

Slang words or expressions are colorful and exaggerated ways of saying ordinary things. For example, if someone is acting strangely, there are many slang expressions to describe that behavior—"He's gone bananas!" or "She's lost her marbles!" or "They must be nuts!" How well can you sling the slang around? Take one minute to test yourself. See how many slang words or expressions you can correctly match to their definitions. Write the letter of the slang in the numbered space next to its definitions.

Slang	Definition
A. Get the lead out.	____1. To reveal the secret.
B. Not playing with a full deck.	____2. To hurry.
C. Chill out.	____3. One who talks too much.
D. Straight from the horse's mouth.	____4. Entirely mistaken.
E. Out in left field.	____5. Nothing.
F. Pull the wool over one's eyes.	____6. Wastebasket.
G. Up a creek without a paddle.	____7. Absent-minded.
H. Two shakes of a lamb's tail.	____8. One's signature.
I. Tickle the ivories.	____9. Neighborhood.
J. There you go.	____10. To admit defeat.
K. Spill the beans.	____11. Troublesome situation.
L. John Hancock.	____12. In a very short time.
M. Hood.	____13. Play the piano.
N. Earbender.	____14. Relax.
O. Circular file.	____15. To deceive.
P. Throw in the towel.	____16. Now you've got it.
Q. Zilch.	____17. From the original source.

BONUS ROUND!

If you finished in less than a minute, write three slang words or expressions which mean "great!" or "very good!"

1._____   2._____   3._____

CHALLENGE #22

DROP-A-LETTER, FIND-A-WORD

Use the first clue to help you figure out the first word in the pair. Then let the second clue help you decide which letter to drop to make a new word. Set the timer for one minute (what else!) and make as many new words as possible before the time is up.

1. A girl getting married is called a _____.
   Drop a letter and go for a _____.

2. Soap and water will get you _____.
   Drop a letter; you're not fat, you're _____!

3. If you want to sweep, use a _____.
   Drop a letter and go to your _____.

4. When you're thirsty get yourself a _____.
   Drop a letter for an ice-skating _____.

5. Before you buy, check the tag for the _____.
   Drop a letter for a white food called _____.

6. To stop the car, step on the _____.
   Drop a letter for a garden _____.

7. When you fly you ride in a big air _____.
   Drop a letter for a walk down the _____.

8. A man wearing armor is called a _____.
   Drop a letter and say "good-_____."

9. Beef and pork are two kinds of _____.
   Drop a letter, now it's time to _____!

10. Boil the water and up rises the _____.
    Drop a letter and cheer for your _____!

11. Look! Up in the sky there's a fluffy white, _____!
    Drop a letter for a noise that is _____.

12. Exercise can make muscles feel _____.
    Drop a letter for some iron _____.

13. A thing that says, "Boo!" is called a _____.
    Drop a letter for a talk show _____.

14. If it's all your fault, then take all the _____.
    Drop a letter for a hurt leg that's _____.

15. If you're hungry, pile food on your _____.
    Drop a letter to be tardy or _____.

16. A party for sleeping is sometimes called "_____."
    Drop a letter and another name for wood is _____.

17. A lobster's hand is called a _____.
    Drop a letter and obey the _____!

18. Hurry now, you're almost _____.
    Drop a letter, this is the last _____!

CHALLENGE #23

JUST SAY NO!

There's a NO in every word in this challenge. Read the definitions and fill in the blanks to complete the NO words. Can you do them all in one minute? Say YES to NO!

1. Opposite of something. N O __ __ __ __ __

2. Handle on a door. __ N O __

3. A banana-shaped boat you paddle. __ __ N O __

4. A prehistoric animal. __ __ N O __ __ __ __

5. It's on your face and smells. N O __ __

6. Opposite of majority. __ __ N O __ __ __ __

7. A judge is called "Your_____." __ __ N O __

8. A short letter. N O __ __

9. White flakes in winter. __ N O __

10. The opposite of major. __ __ N O __

11. The right amount. __ N O __ __ __

12. To bother. __ __ N O __

13. A musical instrument with 88 keys. __ __ __ N O

14. Opposite of sense. N O __ __ __ __ __ __

15. Can't is the contraction. __ __ __ N O __

CHALLENGE #24

MORE REBUS RIDDLES

Each rebus is a riddle. How many riddles can you guess in one minute?

1.
○ ○
○ ○
○ ○

_____

2. RD
OA

_____

3.
L
O
W

_____

4.

ado   ado
ado nothing ado
ado   ado

_____

5.
T
A
L
E

_____

6. POLE
N
W ←→ E
S

_____

7. CYCLE
CYCLE
CYCLE

_____

8.
N   T
NWOT TOWN
O   W
T   N

_____

9.
N
W ←→ E
S
GONE

_____

BONUS ROUND!

If you finished in less than a minute, make up a rebus of your own for extra fun.

CHALLENGE #25

THE NAME OF THE GAME IS NOUN HUNT

A noun is the name of a person, place or thing. Find and underline the nouns in the sentences below. How many can you find in one minute?

1. Corey plays tennis every day.

2. Will he win this tennis match?

3. The score is 15—40, match point.

4. Both players wipe the sweat off their faces with their sleeves.

5. The ground feels hard under Corey's feet.

6. The ball bounces halfway between the baseline and the service line.

7. He swings his racket at the ball and makes contact.

8. "Wow!" Corey thinks to himself. "I won the match!"

BONUS ROUND!

If you finished in less than a minute, find and underline the nouns in this bonus sentence:

Practice is the most important part of every player's game.

CHALLENGE #26

JUST THE OPPOSITE!

All the answers in this challenge are opposites, or antonyms. Use the clues to help you correctly unscramble the letters and spell each opposite word. Write the new words in the spaces provided. How many can you do before one minute is up?

1. Fast   wlos   _____
2. Cold   tho   _____
3. Open   secol   _____
4. Dirty   lanec   _____
5. Soft   drah   _____
6. Empty   lufl   _____
7. Small   gbi   _____
8. happy   das   _____
9. nervous   mcal   _____
10. tall   hrtos   _____
11. fat   htni   _____
12. borrow   nedl   _____
13. take   egiv   _____
14. sour   estwe   _____
15. weak   grtsno   _____
16. awake   peelsa   _____
17. floor   lcneigi   _____
18. love   ehta   _____
19. go   sopt   _____
20. beginning dne   _____
21. death   file   _____
22. good   vile   _____
23. man   nwmoa   _____
24. dark   gtlhi   _____
25. true   slfea   _____

31

CHALLENGE #27

KEN EWE REED?

These sentences are written completely in homonyms. As they are written, they make no sense. How many can you correctly translate into homonyms that will make sense? Set your timer for one minute and begin.

1. Ken ewe reed?

_____

2. Eye sea too oar for flours.

_____

3. Witch which bytes end witch won Ken knot?

_____

4. Dew groan bares grown?

_____

5. Know won nose weather ore knot ate ours past.

_____

6. Hoarse heards flu buy!

_____

7. Won knight eye herd sum belles wring.

_____

32

CHALLENGE #28

-OUGHT OR -AUGHT? YOU OUGHT TO KNOW!

This story ought to be completed in one minute or less. As you read it, fill in the blanks with either *aught* or *ought*. Then read the story again.

C_____ in the Rain

"Oh no!" said Mrs. Minshall's youngest d_____er. "It's starting to rain! We should have br_____ an umbrella."

"Don't worry, dear," her mother said th_____fully. "I never get c_____ without one. If you hold this bag of things I just b_____, I'm sure I'll find the umbrella in my other bag."

"Hurry up, Mom," snapped the d_____er h_____ily. "I t_____ you to be patient," replied Mrs. Minshall. "That tone of voice is not nice. Don't you be a n_____y girl."

"I'm sorry, Mom," replied the girl. The two of them never f_____ about something as silly as getting c_____ in the rain.

In a minute Mrs. Minshall found the thing she s_____. "Here it is!" she smiled happily, holding up the umbrella. "I th_____ I'd find it. And if I didn't I would have b_____ another one!"

BONUS ROUND!
If you finished in less than a minute, try this extra sentence for extra fun:
Vegetarians are t_____ not to sl_____er the animals they've c_____.

33

CHALLENGE #29

MORE ALPHABET SOUP

Each set of initials equals what the number stands for. See how many you can guess before one minute is up.

1. 1001 = A N _____

2. 18 = H on a G C _____

3. 200 = D for P G in M _____

4. 5 = D in a Z C _____

5. 10 = L I B _____

6. 29 = D in F in a L Y _____

7. 57 = H V _____

8. 2 = W on a B _____

9. 9 = I in a B G _____

10. 32 = DF at which W F _____

11. 50 = S on the U.S. F _____

12. 2 = S to E S _____

CHALLENGE #30

WORD PYRAMIDS

Use the clues to help you fill in the blanks. Start at the top of each word pyramid. Add one letter in each step down. How many word pyramids can you build in a minute?

G
___ ___
Ready, set, ____!

___ ___ ___
Already received.

___ ___ ___ ___
Farm or mountain animal.

___ ___ ___ ___ ___
Think about with mean pleasure.

O
___ ___
Either, ___

___ ___ ___
Rowing tool.

___ ___ ___ ___
Wild pig.

___ ___ ___ ___ ___
Wooden plank.

T
___ ___
Homonym for two or too.

___ ___ ___
2,000 pounds = 1 ____

___ ___ ___ ___
Musical sound or make a muscle.

___ ___ ___ ___ ___
A rock.

H
___ ___
A laugh.

___ ___ ___
Sandwich meat.

___ ___ ___ ___
Hurt.

___ ___ ___ ___ ___
Small lucky symbol.

H
___ ___
Him.

___ ___ ___
She.

___ ___ ___ ___
Listen and catch sound.

___ ___ ___ ___ ___
Valentine shape.

A
___ ___
One ___ a time.

___ ___ ___
Hunger solution.

___ ___ ___ ___
Sit on it.

___ ___ ___ ___ ___
Perspire.

CHALLENGE #31

SPELL CHECK

Find the word in each group that is spelled correctly. Circle the letter in front of the correctly spelled word in each row. Set your timer for one minute and begin.

1. a. atic   b. attick   c. attic   d. adik
2. a. canoo   b. canue   c. cano   d. canoe
3. a. answer   b. ansur   c. anser   d. ansure
4. a. lauf   b. laff   c. laugh   d. laffe
5. a. prety   b. pritty   c. priddy   d. pretty
6. a. sootcase   b. suitcase   c. suitcays   d. sutcase
7. a. scard   b. scaired   c. scared   d. skared
8. a. ekwel   b. equal   c. eekwall   d. eakqual
9. a. senior   b. senure   c. seenior   d. seanure
10. a. acke   b. ake   c. ache   d. eake
11. a. recipee   b. resipe   c. ressipee   d. recipe
12. a. salid   b. saled   c. salad   d. salade
13. a. yaght   b. yacht   c. yaught   d. yaht
14. a. fasten   b. fassen   c. fastin   d. fassin
15. a. antike   b. anteque   c. antique   d. anteek
16. a. plummer   b. plomber   c. plumger   d. plumber
17. a. gess   b. gues   c. guess   d. gesse
18. a. twelth   b. twelfth   c. twellfth   d. twelphth
19. a. pome   b. poam   c. powem   d. poem
20. a. scissers   b. scissors   c. scizzors   d. siccors

36

CHALLENGE #32

FIND THE FRAGMENTS

Every sentence should tell a complete thought. A fragment does not tell a complete thought. Read the sentences below. Set the timer for one minute. How many sentences and fragments can you correctly identify in the time allowed? Write S for sentence and F for fragment in the space before each group of words.

___ 1. Kip plays shortstop on his school's baseball team.
___ 2. Sewing with a needle and thread.
___ 3. Lauren on the roller coaster.
___ 4. My cousin and I.
___ 5. Go to your room!
___ 6. Empty pockets, empty wallets.
___ 7. All the way home.
___ 8. The fun is just beginning.
___ 9. Call me in the morning.
___ 10. Stop!
___ 11. Never say never.
___ 12. The sled in the snow.
___ 13. Some say thirteen is an unlucky number.
___ 14. It isn't.
___ 15. Who wants more?
___ 16. Music on the radio.
___ 17. Change the channel.
___ 18. Why do you cry?
___ 19. If the shoe fits, wear it.
___ 20. A sentence has a subject and a predicate.

CHALLENGE #33

COMMAS, THE PAUSES THAT REFRESH

Commas make a reader pause when reading. Use a comma to separate items in dates and items in addresses. Use a comma after *yes, no, ah, oh,* and *well* when these words begin a sentence. Use these rules to help you correctly place commas where they belong in the sentences below. Set the timer for one minute and begin.

1. Yes I did say I'd meet him on July 25 1999.
2. I sent a letter to Mr. Coleman's house at 25 Pine Street Evansville Virginia.
3. Oh I wouldn't be too sure about that!
4. Well we missed the boat.
5. No we don't plan to move from Boston Massachusetts to New York New York.
6. Ah you mean you remember the parade on Monday July 4 1985?
7. So do you think your team will win this year?
8. Philadelphia Pennsylvania has many sights to see.
9. Yes we are planning a reunion on December 7 2002.
10. Oh who can possibly remember all the names of all the states?

BONUS ROUND!
If you finished in less than a minute, add the commas to these sentences for extra fun.

My grandmother was born February 16 1938 in Portland Maine. Oh how she loves that town!
"Yes I think this is the best place in the world!" she says.

Challenge #34

Action Verbs for Active People

Words that add action to a sentence are called action verbs. These verbs tell about action you can see (for example: run, jump, laugh) and about action you cannot see (for example: like, think, believe). Set the timer for one minute. Then underline the action verbs in the sentences below.

1. Martin Luther King, Jr. dreamed of freedom for all people.

2. Thomas Jefferson wrote the Declaration of Independence.

3. Albert Einstein thought too much in class.

4. Mark Twain worked on a riverboat on the Mississippi River.

5. Even though she was blind, Helen Keller was able to read, write, and finish college.

6. Grandma Moses painted until her hands were too weak to hold a brush.

7. Wolfgang Mozart composed music when he was five years old.

8. Marco Polo traveled from Venice to China.

9. Eleanor Roosevelt carried the message of world peace wherever she spoke.

10. Chief Joseph wished his people did not have to fight for their land.

11. Harry Houdini made his audiences believe in magic.

12. Benjamin Franklin taught himself algebra, geometry, science, logic, writing, grammar, and five foreign languages.

CHALLENGE #35

MAGIC SQUARES

The answers in these crosswords are the same across and down. Read the clues and fill in as many Magic Squares as you can in one minute.

1. Spoiled child.
2. Wealthy.
3. A pain.
4. Opposite of now.

1. A present.
2. A thought.
3. To touch.
4. Opposite of short.

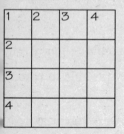

1. Winter white stuff.
2. Three times three.
3. One less than twice.
4. Seven days equal one.

1. _____, crackle, pop!
2. What you call yourself.
3. Prayer ending.
4. Ink-filled writing instruments

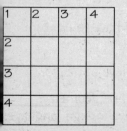

CHALLENGE #36

STATE STUMPER

The names of 15 states are hidden in the sentences below. Underline them as you find them. Your one minute time limit begins right . . . NOW!

1. Is that terrible bore gone yet?

2. "Mama, I need a new bicycle," said the little boy.

3. We saw the color ad on the front page of the newspaper.

4. "Oh, I only like mustard on hot dogs," my uncle said.

5. Put a ham in the shopping cart.

6. I see the lovely miss is sipping soda through a straw.

7. Will Al ask a doctor about that pain in his neck?

8. I sure miss our incredible teacher, don't you?

9. Where did Mary land her plane after the transatlantic flight?

10. The new beach has a Wade Law, a Read Law, and a Sand Castle Law.

11. I want a large or giant box of chocolates to share with my friends.

12. Before I connect, I cut the wires and tape the ends.

13. Ken, tuck your shirt in please!

14. If Lori dares to speak out in class, she'll be sent to the office again.

15. "I feel ill," I noisily complained to the flight attendant.

CHALLENGE #37

ORDER IN THE ALPHABET!

Putting words in alphabetical order can be tricky. Set the timer for one minute, then see how many groups of words below you can put in alphabetical order before your time is up. Number the words in the order you choose.

1
___ flies
___ dirt
___ files
___ deal
___ field
___ drip

2
___ sponge
___ squash
___ summer
___ spoken
___ snow
___ swing

3
___ talent
___ tall
___ talk
___ telephone
___ under
___ silly

4
___ bones
___ broken
___ about
___ above
___ best
___ bacon

5
___ chapter
___ calendar
___ chord
___ chance
___ dreary
___ dresser

6
___ open
___ pencil
___ peninsula
___ opera
___ operation
___ odor

7
___ match
___ name
___ nurse
___ mound
___ movie
___ mark

8
___ defeat
___ deduct
___ defense
___ detail
___ delete
___ delight

BONUS ROUND!

If you finished in less than a minute, try these for extra fun. If you alphabetize them correctly you'll read a surprise message!

___ learn
___ all
___ well
___ kids
___ very

CHALLENGE #38

START MAKING SENSE

The sentences below are nonsense sentences. Set the timer for one minute. Then rearrange the words in each sentence to make sensible sentences. Rewrite them on the lines given.

1. for a is Superman job this!

_____

2. sound the to listen waves the of.

_____

3. want grow you you to up when what do be?

_____

4. is hand cookie the my jar in stuck.

_____

5. hear my I elephants when cover I snore ears!

_____

6. parties at pops Peter balloons.

_____

7. secret can keep you a?

_____

A LETTER HOME

Here's a letter from a camper at Camp Cap-and-Punc. The capitalization and punctuation marks are missing. Set your timer for one minute, then start adding capital letters and the correct punctuation. How many corrections can you make before the time is up?

dear mom and dad

  i am in my cabin here at camp cap-and-punc so far i have been bitten by three mosquitoes two spiders and one red ant it only hurts when i laugh

  my counselors name is chris he calls me spot because i have so many bug bites all over me i like having a nickname i just wish it was another name besides spot

  the food here is worse than i thought it would be they say t will start tasting better to us after a couple of days i guess f i get hungry enough ill eat anything

  well i really miss you guys and i hope you send me a care package real soon send brownies chips gum and bug spray

                         your happy camper

                         jamie

CHALLENGE #40

ADVERB WORD SEARCH

Adverbs are words that tell how, where, or when. Many adverbs are formed by adding *-ly* to an adjective, but not all. Using the adverb list here, how many can you find and circle in one minute?

Adverb List:

carelessly	carefully	slowly	down	early	often
today	nowhere	outside	quickly	fast	easily
here	tomorrow	badly	near	loudly	well
then	up	far	now		

```
C A R E L E S S L Y F
B A D L Y R T H E N A
Y L R A E A S I L Y S
H E R E J E W E L L T
N O W K F N O D O W N
Y L K C I U Q W B Y E
P O L I T E L Y D L T
R Q V S Z Y X L M D F
E A I X T O D A Y U O
G D F W O R R O M O T
E R E H W O N U P L X
```

45

CHALLENGE #41

ODD WORD OUT

In each group of words there is one word that does not belong. Find and circle the letter in front of the word you think should be removed. Set your timer for one minute and start taking the odd words out.

1. a) breakfast   b) lunch   c) grapefruit   d) dinner
2. a) socks   b) boots   c) shoes   d) gloves
3. a) television   b) movies   c) radio   d) video
4. a) spinach   b) bananas   c) asparagus   d) artichokes
5. a) New York   b) Ohio   c) Los Angeles   d) California
6. a) lake   b) river   c) stream   d) puddle
7. a) dog   b) poodle   c) Dalmatian   d) collie
8. a) rain   b) weather   c) sleet   d) snow
9. a) nine   b) four   c) six   d) eight
10. a) cow   b) pig   c) elephant   d) sheep
11. a) ears   b) leg   c) eyes   d) nose
12. a) square   b) rectangle   c) triangle   d) angle
13. a) trumpet   b) banjo   c) guitar   d) ukelele
14. a) happy   b) tears   c) sad   d) angry
15. a) Mars   b) Venus   c) Moon   d) Earth
16. a) Ford   b) Toyota   c) Dodge   d) Chevrolet
17. a) workbench   b) hammer   c) drill   d) screwdriver
18. a) English   b) Science   c) French   d) Spanish
19. a) Carolyn   b) Carl   c) Chad   d) Charles
20. a) bite   b) bark   c) chirp   d) purr

BONUS ROUND!

If you finished in less than a minute, try this for extra fun!

   a) ha ha   b) huff puff   c) tee hee   d) ho ho

CHALLENGE #42

RUN-IN WITH RUN-ONS

A run-on sentence has two or more sentences about different thoughts written as one single sentence. How many run-on sentences can you correctly identify below in one minute? In the space before each group of words, write S for correct sentences and R if it is a run-on sentence.

_____1. Charlie loved the chocolate factory the chocolate was the best he'd ever tasted.

_____2. If Anne Shirley had something on her mind, she always made a point of speaking up.

_____3. Whatever made Tom Sawyer decide to go in that cave he should have stayed at home.

_____4. When Maniac Magee ran in a race he always won.

_____5. The lost girls were shipwrecked on an island they used shells to keep track of how many days they were lost.

_____6. Did the Banks children think Mary Poppins was strange?

_____7. Dorothy knew she wasn't in Kansas anymore the straw man talked to her!

_____8. Dr. Frankenstein created a monster in his laboratory.

_____9. Sherlock Holmes solves mysteries his good friend Watson helps.

_____10. Didn't Scarlett O'Hara go back to Tara after Atlanta burned?

_____11. Living alone didn't bother Pippi Longstocking her father was somewhere at sea.

_____12. A little bit of magic seems to help Mrs. Piggle-Wiggle get through the day.

_____13. Charlotte thought Wilbur was a very special pig Wilbur was her best friend.

CHALLENGE #43

BOOK TITLE TIME

Capitalize the first word, the last word, and any other important words in a title. Set the timer for one minute and begin. Underline each letter you think should be capitalized.

1. little house on the prairie
2. frog and toad together
3. the wizard of oz
4. cloudy with a chance of meatballs
5. alice in wonderland
6. the phantom tollbooth
7. gone with the wind
8. treasure island
9. lassie come home
10. the whipping boy
11. horton hears a who
12. a light in the attic
13. lord of the flies
14. phantom of the opera
15. the lion, the witch, and the wardrobe

BONUS ROUND!

If you finished in less than a minute, try this for extra fun!

the cat in the hat comes back

CHALLENGE #44

KNOW YOUR PLURALS

Plural means "more than one." Write the plural on the line next to each word. Set your timer for one minute and begin.

1. goose _____
2. train_____
3. knife_____
4. foot_____
5. sheep_____
6. leaf_____
7. boy_____
8. mouse_____
9. key_____
10. box_____
11. wolf_____
12. man_____
13. potato_____
14. porch_____
15. ghost_____
16. glass_____
17. calf_____
18. spy_____
19. baby_____
20. deer_____

BONUS ROUND!

If you finished in less than a minute try these for extra fun!

scissors_____   Chinese_____

salmon_____

Challenge #45

Word Holiday

Ready for a word holiday? Here it is! How many words can you find in the word HOLIDAY? Set your timer for one minute. Then see how many words you can make using the letters that spell HOLIDAY.

HOLIDAY

1._____   2._____

3._____   4._____

5._____   6._____

7._____   8._____

9._____   10._____

11._____   12._____

13._____   14._____

15._____   16._____

CHALLENGE #46

OU OR *OW*? YOU DECIDE!

How well do you know when to use *ou* or *ow*? Test yourself here. How many words can you spell correctly in one minute? Fill in the blanks with either *ou* or *ow* to complete the words.

fr_____n	sc_____t	gr_____nd
p_____nce	all_____	p_____der
f_____nd	sh_____er	l_____d
sl_____ch	fl_____r	t_____er
spr_____t	t_____el	cr_____d
ch_____der	b_____nce	bl_____se
s_____nd	_____r	c_____nt
t_____r	p_____r	st_____t
tr_____sers	m_____se	cl_____n
c_____ard	f_____l	v_____el

BONUS ROUND!

If you finished in less than a minute try these for extra fun!

cr_____ch   sc_____l   c_____ch

51

CHALLENGE #47

S-PECIALLY FOR YOU!

Did you know there are more words in the English language beginning with the letter *s* than any other letter? Set your timer for one minute. Then start writing as many *s*-words as you can think of. How many can you write before your time is up?

S Words

1. _____
2. _____
3. _____
4. _____
5. _____
6. _____
7. _____
8. _____
9. _____
10. _____
11. _____
12. _____
13. _____
14. _____
15. _____
16. _____
17. _____
18. _____
19. _____
20. _____
21. _____
22. _____
23. _____
24. _____
25. _____
26. _____
27. _____
28. _____
29. _____
30. _____

BONUS ROUND!

If you finished in less than a minute, keep going!

CHALLENGE #48

FOREIGN AFFAIRS

The names of 15 countries are hidden in the sentences below. Underline them as you find them. Your one minute time limit begins right . . . NOW!

1. Builders agree cement is the best material to use for foundations.

2. The doctors think if there is a germ anywhere it will spread disease.

3. Mrs. Wolff ran centers for daycare.

4. Yes, pains come and go when athletes are in training.

5. If you have swollen glands you should stay home from school.

6. Is it Al Young's fault that we missed the bus?

7. When the car crashed, a tire landed on the side of the road.

8. If you point at us, we deny any wrongdoing.

9. The bear cub acted friendly.

10. The beard on his chin actually makes him look younger!

11. This will show a less complicated method for solving problems.

12. Russ, I always wanted to grow roses in my garden.

13. The sparkle in diamonds reminds me of stars in the sky.

14. Can a day go by without the weatherman predicting rain?

15. When the school bully arrived I ran away.

CHALLENGE #49

TWIN-LETTER WORDS

The words below begin and end with the same two letters in the same order. The first and last pair of letters have been left out. Use the clues to help you. Then, set your timer for one minute and begin filling in the missing letters. In each case, if you get the first two letters, you have the last two.

__ __ U R __ __   Place of worship.

__ __ M A __ __   Salad ingredient.

__ __ A D A C __ __   Pain in the cranium.

__ __ A S __ __   Mistake remover.

__ __ N __ __   Smell is one.

__ __ I T __ __   Corrected, as in a composition or manuscript.

__ __ I __ __   Vegetable to cry for.

__ __ T A T __ __   Homes of the rich and famous.

__ __ Y L I __ __   Hair designer.

__ __ G I B __ __   Written clearly; readable.

CHALLENGE #50

THE END PUZZLE

The END is in sight in every word in this challenge. Read the definitions to help you complete each END word. Remember END isn't always at the END. How many can you complete before one minute has come to an END?

1. __ END — To mail something.

2. __ END __ __ — Opposite of tough.

3. __ __ __ END — To argue on the side of someone.

4. __ __ __ END — To count on someone.

5. __ END __ __ — Opposite of borrower.

6. __ __ __ END — To insult.

7. __ __ __ __ END — To make believe.

8. __ __ END — To add to or change, as in the Constitution.

9. __ __ __ END — A pal.

10. __ __ __ END __ __ — All the months are on it.

11. __ __ __ __ __ END — Extra bonus.

12. __ END — To repair as in sewing.

13. END __ __ __ __ __ __ __ — Species which is almost extinct.

14. __ __ __ __ END __ — Video game system.

15. __ __ END — A fad or fashion.

BONUS ROUND!

If you finished in less than a minute, END with these END words!

__ __ __ END — To move upward.

__ __ END — To mix together.

__ __ __ __ __ __ END — To capture or catch up with.

55

ANSWERS

CHALLENGE #1

1. stare; 2. bear; 3. bee; 4. sea; 5. grown; 6. loan; 7. vein; 8. mane; 9. week; 10. peak; 11. steak; 12. break; 13. pane; 14. reign; 15. hour; 16. flour; 17. dye; 18. by; 19. due; 20. ewe; 21. wear; 22. hair; 23. haul; 24. bawl; 25. flue; 26. too; 27. knight; 28. write; 29. won; 30. sun; 31. hoarse; 32. coarse; 33. hear; 34. pier; 35. whole; 36. role; 37. air; 38. pear; 39. pail; 40. sail.
Bonus Round: 41. kernel; 42. minor.

CHALLENGE #2

1. let's; 2. he's; 3. they've; 4. weren't; 5. here's; 6. she's; 7. they're; 8. what's; 9. hasn't; 10. we'll; 11. that's; 12. don't; 13. can't; 14. I'd; 15. they'll; 16. you'll; 17. I've; 18. it's; 19. you're; 20. didn't; 21. she'll; 22. you've; 23. aren't; 24. there's; 25. I'll; 26. isn't; 27. who's; 28. won't; 29. wasn't; 30. she'd; 31. doesn't; 32. he'll.
Bonus Round: 33. have not; 34. you will; 35. we have; 36. could not; 37. they would; 38. should not.

CHALLENGE #3

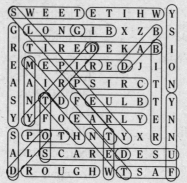

CHALLENGE #4

Answers will vary. Possible answers include:
ate, bait, bate, crate, date, eight, fate, freight, gait, gate, grate, hate, Kate, late, mate, Nate, pate, plait, plate, rate, skate, slate, state, straight, strait, trait, wait, weight, abate, await, bookplate, checkmate, collate, create, dictate, donate, elate, estate, frustrate, graduate, inflate, inmate, irate, locate, mandate, mismate, mutate, narrate, ornate, primate, probate, relate, stagnate, vacate, recapitulate, misappropriate.
Bonus Round: Possible answers include: best, lest, test, dressed, confessed, nest, pest, guest, jest, west, zest, behest, stressed.

CHALLENGE #5

Answers will vary. Possible answers include:
A. aisle; B. dumb; C. czar; D. Wednesday; E. snore; F. stuff; G. gnu; H. honest; I. aim; J. San Juan; K. know; L. could; M. mnemonic; N. hymn; O. rough; P. psychology; Q. acquire; R. Mrs.; S. island; T. often; U. gauge;

V. no answer!; W. write; X. xylophone; Y. gray; Z. Czechoslovakia.
(If you found a V word, excellent!)

CHALLENGE #6

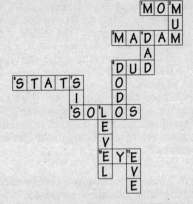

CHALLENGE #7

1. neither; 2. grieve; 3. view; 4. brief; 5. chief; 6. height; 7. friend; 8. believe;
9. conceit; 10. beige; 11. relief; 12. ceiling; 13. mischief; 14. piece; 15. seize;
16. forfeit; 17. protein; 18. ancient; 19. sleight; 20. deceive; 21. receipt;
22. shield; 23. caffeine; 24. priest; 25. thief; 26. reign; 27. field; 28. hygiene;
29. siege; 30. sovereign; 31. glacier; 32. science; 33. species; 34. heir;
35. reindeer; 36. weight; 37. neighbor; 38. cashier; 39. conscience; 40. grief;
41. besiege; 42. sieve; 43. weird; 44. belief; 45. pierce; 46. shriek; 47. frontier;
48. efficient; 49. counterfeit; 50. achieve.

CHALLENGE #8

1. crossroads; 2. six feet underground; 3. touchdown; 4. sign on the dotted
line; 5. square meal; 6. six of one, half a dozen of another; 7. a hole in one;
8. make a mountain out of a molehill; 9. Key West.

CHALLENGE #9

AL; AK; AZ; AR; CA; CO; CT; DE; FL; GA; HI; ID; IL; IN; IA; KS; KY; LA; ME;
MD; MA; MI; MN; MS; MO; MT; NE; NV; NH; NJ; NM; NY; NC; ND; OH; OK;
OR; PA; RI; SC; SD; TN; TX; UT; VT; VA; WA; WV; WI; WY.
Bonus Round: CZ; DC; GU; PR; VI.

CHALLENGE #10

The Thing in the Lake

   On Saturday, July 14, Mom, Dad, and I drove to Sebago Lake. I was hoping
the Morris family and their big bully of a son, Butch, wouldn't be there
waiting for us. Well, Butch was there all right, but so was something else.
Everybody was talking about the monster in the lake.

   "Sheriff Johnson and his deputy stayed up all night watching for it," said
Butch's Aunt Harriet. "They're calling the thing Nessie, after the Loch Ness
Monster. If you ask me, I think it's just a big old carp."

   "No child of mine is going to be bait for a lake monster," Mom told Dad. "I think we should get in the car and go back home to our house on Pine Street in our safe little town of Pine Bluffs, Massachusetts. The only monsters there are the dust balls under the bed!"

Just as I was about to complain, I turned for one last look at Sebago Lake. Guess what I saw waving at me from out in the middle of the lake? Butch Morris, who else? It was all his idea of one big joke. The laugh was on him, though, because right behind him something else was waving, too. It was Nessie, the thing in the lake! When Butch saw the monster behind him, he swam ashore as fast as he could.

Butch and his family left and never came back to the lake. As for Mom, Dad, and me, we stayed and had the best summer ever. Butch's aunt was right. The "monster" was just a big fish. It's in an aquarium in Boston now. Thanks to the monster, the really scary thing in the lake is gone! Bye, Butch. I don't miss you at all!

CHALLENGE #11

1. armchair; downpour; bareback; earthworm; chairperson.
2. teardrop; birthplace; nametag; blackbird; worldwide.
3. scorecard; knapsack; knockout; newspaper; shipwreck.
4. textbook; broomstick; flagpole; suitcase; moonlight.
5. teamwork; streetcar; newborn; chalkboard; playmate.

CHALLENGE #12

who	rat (art)	any (nay)
cat (act)	ore	had
box	car (arc)	ten (net)
and (Dan)	bit	bun (nub)
lip	old	hot
are (ear)	hat	too
put	pat (tap)	how (who)
bus (sub)	bug	fed
mom	tub (but)	dig
two (tow)	gap	bee
nut	for	nap (pan)
oak	far	eye
one	fun	oar
hop	gun (gnu)	zoo
sew	use (sue)	map
man	she	bad (dab)

Bonus Round: hand, head, hair, help.

CHALLENGE #13

Answers will vary. Possible answers include:
bat; car; heat; far; ant; Ben; plan; ten; rest; hoe; west; few; pear; pal; sale; law; raw; how; low; ten; end.

CHALLENGE #14

1. hat; 2. painting; 3. swimming; 4. floor; 5. empty; 6. vegetable; 7 taste; 8. enclosing; 9. water; 10. ship; 11. glove; 12. down; 13. eleventh; 14. sled; 15. thermometer.

CHALLENGE #15

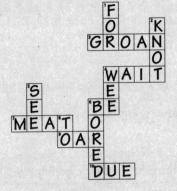

CHALLENGE #16

1. "Did you hear about the three holes in the ground?" Sam asked.
2. "Well, well, well," John answered.
3. Carolyn wondered, "Is anyone going to notice that I got new braces?"
4. "Did you get a new haircut?" John asked Carolyn when she arrived at school the next day.
5. "Look!" shouted my little brother. "The ice cream man forgot to close the freezer door on his truck!"
6. I knew there was only one thing to do. "Hey, ice cream man," I called after him, "you forgot to close the freezer door!"
7. "Some people believe that pepper makes a person sneeze," the teacher said, sprinkling the black grains in her hand. "I myself have never believed that."
8. "Achoo!" she sneezed. "Achoo! Achoo! Achoo!"

CHALLENGE #17

1. 26 = Letters of the Alphabet; 2. 4 and 20 = Blackbirds Baked in a Pie; 3. 9 = Planets in the Solar System; 4. 24 = Hours in a Day; 5. 12 = Months in the Year; 6. 7 = Days in a Week; 7. 4 = Quarts in a Gallon; 8. 13 = Stripes on the U.S. Flag; 9. 52 (53) = Cards in a Deck (with the Joker); 10. 90 = Degrees in a Right Angle; 11. 11 = Players on a Football Team; 12. 3 = Blind Mice "See How They Run."

CHALLENGE #18

Blind as a bat; Dead as a doornail; Cold as ice; Flat as a pancake; Quiet as a mouse; Snug as a bug in a rug; Old as the hills; Sly as a fox; Neat as a pin; Light as a feather; Fit as a fiddle; Busy as a bee; Slow as molasses; Fat as a pig; Proud as a peacock; Nutty as a fruitcake; Sharp as a tack.

CHALLENGE #19

There are no *e's* in the whole paragraph.

CHALLENGE #20

1. F; 2. T; 3. F; 4. F; 5. T; 6. F; 7. T; 8. F; 9. F; 10. F; 11. F; 12. F; 13. T; 14. F; 15. T; 16. F; 17. F; 18. F; 19. T; 20. T; 21. F; 22. F; 23. T; 24. T; 25. T; 26. F; 27. T; 28. F; 29. F; 30. F; 31. T; 32. F; 33. F.
Bonus Round: 34. F; 35. T.

CHALLENGE #21

1-K; 2-A; 3-N; 4-E; 5-Q; 6-O; 7-B; 8-L; 9-M; 10-P; 11-G; 12-H; 13-I; 14-C; 15-F; 16-J; 17-D.
Bonus Round: Possible answers are: cool, awesome, sweet.

CHALLENGE #22

1. bride-ride; 2. clean-lean; 3. broom-room; 4. drink-rink; 5. price-rice; 6. brake-rake; 7. plane-lane; 8. knight-night; 9. meat-eat; 10. steam-team; 11. cloud-loud; 12. sore-ore; 13. ghost-host; 14. blame-lame; 15. plate-late; 16. slumber-lumber; 17. claw-law; 18. done-one.

CHALLENGE #23

1. NOthing; 2. kNOb; 3. caNOe; 4. diNOsaur; 5. NOse; 6. miNOrity; 7. hoNOr; 8. NOte; 9. sNOw; 10. miNOr; 11. eNOugh; 12. anNOy; 13. piaNO; 14. NOnsense; 15. canNOt.

CHALLENGE #24

1. cheery Os; 2. fork in the road; 3. low down; 4. much ado about nothing; 5.tall tale; 6. North Pole; 7. tricycle; 8. uptown, downtown; 9. gone south

CHALLENGE #25

1. Corey, tennis, day; 2. he, match; 3. score, point; 4. players, sweat, faces, sleeves; 5. ground, Corey's feet; 6. ball, baseline, line; 7. He, racquet, ball, contact; 8. Corey, himself, I, match.
Bonus Round: Practice, part, player's game

CHALLENGE #26

1. slow; 2. hot; 3. close; 4. clean; 5. hard; 6. full; 7. big; 8. sad; 9. calm; 10. short; 11. thin; 12. lend; 13. give; 14. sweet; 15. strong; 16. asleep; 17. ceiling; 18. hate; 19. stop; 20. end; 21. life; 22. evil; 23. woman; 24. light; 25. false.

CHALLENGE #27

1. Can you read? 2. I see two or four flowers. 3. Which witch bites and which one cannot? 4. Do grown bears groan? 5. No one knows whether or not eight hours passed. 6. Horse herds flew by! 7. One night I heard some bells ring.

CHALLENGE #28

Caught; daughter; brought; thoughtfully; caught; bought; daughter; haughtily; taught; naughty; fought; caught; sought; thought; bought. Bonus Round: taught; slaughter; caught.

CHALLENGE #29

1. 1001 = Arabian Nights; 2. 18 = Holes on a Golf Course; 3. 200 = Dollars for Passing Go in Monopoly; 4. 5 = Digits in a Zip Code; 5. 10 = Little Indian Boys; 6. 29 = Days in February in a Leap Year; 7. 57 = Heinz Varieties; 8. 2 = Wheels on a Bicycle; 9. 9 = Innings in a Baseball Game; 10. 32 = Degrees Fahrenheit at which Water Freezes; 11. 50 = Stars on the U. S. Flag; 12. 2 = Sides to Every Story.

CHALLENGE #30

G—go, got, goat, gloat ; O—or, oar, boar, board; T—to, ton, tone, stone; H—ha, ham, harm, charm; H—he, her, hear, heart; A-at, eat, seat, sweat.

CHALLENGE #31

1. c; 2. d; 3. a; 4. c; 5. d; 6. b; 7. c; 8. b; 9. a; 10. c; 11. d; 12. c; 13. b; 14. a; 15. c; 16. d; 17. c; 18. b; 19. d; 20. b.

CHALLENGE #32

1. S; 2. F; 3. F; 4. F; 5. S; 6. F; 7. F; 8. S; 9. S; 10. S; 11. S; 12. F; 13. S; 14. S; 15. S; 16. F; 17. S; 18. S; 19. S; 20. S.

CHALLENGE #33

1. Yes, I did say I'd meet him on July 25, 1999.
2. I sent a letter to Mr. Coleman's house at 25 Pine Street, Evansville, Virginia.
3. Oh, I wouldn't be too sure about that!
4. Well, we missed the boat.
5. No, we don't plan to move from Boston, Massachusetts to New York, New York.
6. Ah, you mean you remember the parade on Monday, July 4, 1985?
7. So, do you think your team will win this year?
8. Philadelphia, Pennsylvania has many sights to see.
9. Yes, we are planning a reunion on December 7, 2002.
10. Oh, who can possibly remember all the names of all the states?
Bonus Round: My grandmother was born February 16, 1938 in Portland, Maine. Oh, how she loves that town!
"Yes, I think this is the best place in the world!" she says.

CHALLENGE #34

1. dreamed; 2. wrote; 3. thought; 4. worked; 5. read, write, finish; 6. painted, hold; 7. composed; 8. traveled ; 9. carried, spoke; 10. wished, fight; 11. made, believe; 12. taught.

61

CHALLENGE #35

	1	2	3	4
1	B	R	A	T
2	R	I	C	H
3	A	C	H	E
4	T	H	E	N

	1	2	3	4
1	G	I	F	T
2	I	D	E	A
3	F	E	E	L
4	T	A	L	L

	1	2	3	4
1	S	N	O	W
2	N	I	N	E
3	O	N	C	E
4	W	E	E	K

	1	2	3	4
1	S	N	A	P
2	N	A	M	E
3	A	M	E	N
4	P	E	N	S

CHALLENGE #36

1. <u>bore gone</u>; 2. Ma<u>ma, I need</u>; 3. <u>color ad on</u>; 4. "<u>Oh, I o</u>nly; 5. <u>put a ham</u>;
6. <u>miss is sipping</u>; 7. <u>Al ask a</u>; 8. <u>miss our i</u>ncredible; 9. <u>Mary land</u>;
10. Wa<u>de law, a Re</u>ad law; 11. lar<u>ge or gia</u>nt; 12. <u>connect, I cut</u>;
13. <u>Ken, tuck y</u>our; 14. <u>If Lori da</u>tes; 15. <u>ill," I</u> noisily.

CHALLENGE #37

1. deal, dirt, drip, field, files, flies; 2. snow, spoken, sponge, squash, summer, swing; 3. silly, talent, talk, tall, telephone, under; 4. about, above, bacon, best, bones, broken; 5. calendar, chance, chapter, chord, dreary, dresser; 6. odor, open, opera, operation, pencil, peninsula; 7. mark, match, mound, movie, name, nurse; 8. deduct, defeat, defense, delete, delight, detail.
Bonus Round: All kids learn very well.

CHALLENGE #38

1. This is a job for Superman! 2. Listen to the sound of the waves. 3. What do you want to be when you grow up? 4. My hand is stuck in the cookie jar. 5. I cover my ears when I hear elephants snore! 6. Peter pops balloons at parties. 7. Can you keep a secret?

CHALLENGE #39

Dear Mom and Dad,

I am in my cabin here at Camp Cap-and-Punc. So far I have been bitten by three mosquitoes, two spiders, and one red ant. It only hurts when I laugh.

My counselor's name is Chris. He calls me "Spot" because I have so many bug bites all over me. I like having a nickname. I just wish it was another name besides "Spot."

The food here is worse than I thought it would be. They say it will start tasting better to us after a couple of days. I guess if I get hungry enough I'll eat anything.

Well, I really miss you guys, and I hope you send me a care package real soon. Send brownies, chips, gum, and bug spray.

      Your happy camper,
      Jamie

CHALLENGE # 40 ADVERB WORD SEARCH

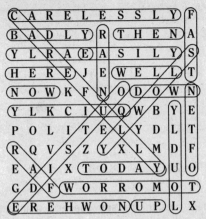

```
C A R E L E S S L Y F
B A D L Y R T H E N A
Y L R A E A S I L Y S
H E R E J E W E L L T
N O W K F N O D O W N
Y L K C I U Q W B Y E
P O L I T E L Y D L T
R Q V S Z Y X L M D F
E A I X T O D A Y U O
G D F W O R R O M O T
E R E H W O N U P L X
```

CHALLENGE #41
1. grapefruit; 2. gloves; 3. radio; 4. bananas; 5. Los Angeles; 6. puddle;
7. dog; 8. weather; 9. nine; 10. elephant; 11. leg; 12. angle; 13. trumpet;
14. tears; 15. Moon; 16. Toyota; 17. workbench; 18. Science; 19. Carolyn;
20. bite.
Bonus Round: huff puff

CHALLENGE #42
1. R; 2. S; 3. R; 4. S; 5. R; 6. S; 7. R; 8. S; 9. R; 10. S; 11. R; 12. S; 13. R

CHALLENGE #43
1. Little House on the Prairie; 2. Frog and Toad Together; 3. The Wizard of
Oz; 4. Cloudy with a Chance of Meatballs; 5. Alice in Wonderland;
6. The Phantom Tollbooth; 7. Gone with the Wind; 8. Treasure Island;
9. Lassie Come Home; 10. The Whipping Boy; 11. Horton Hears a Who;
12. A Light in the Attic; 13. Lord of the Flies; 14. Phantom of the Opera;
15. The Lion, the Witch, and the Wardrobe
Bonus Round: The Cat in the Hat Comes Back

CHALLENGE #44
1. geese; 2. trains; 3. knives; 4. feet; 5. sheep; 6. leaves; 7. boys; 8. mice;
9. keys; 10. boxes; 11. wolves; 12. men; 13. potatoes; 14. porches; 15. ghosts;
16. glasses; 17. calves; 18. spies; 19. babies; 20. deer.
Bonus Round: scissors, Chinese, salmon.

CHALLENGE #45
Answers will vary. Possible answers include:
ahoy, aid, ail, daily, day, dial, doily, had, hail, hay, hi, hid, hold, holy, I, lad,
laid, lay, lid, oh, oil, oily, old.

CHALLENGE #46

frown, scout, ground, pounce, allow, powder, found, shower, loud, slouch, flour, tower, sprout, towel, crowd, chowder, bounce, blouse, sound, our, count, tour, pour, stout, trousers, mouse, clown, coward, foul, vowel.
Bonus Round: crouch, scowl, couch

CHALLENGE #47

Look in the *s* section of a dictionary for a complete selection of *s*-words.

CHALLENGE #48

1. a<u>gree ce</u>ment; 2. <u>germ any</u>where; 3. Wolf<u>f ran ce</u>nters; 4. Ye<u>s, pain</u>s;
5. swollen glands; 6. <u>it Al You</u>ng's; 7. <u>tire la</u>nded; 8. u<u>s, we den</u>y;
9. <u>cub a</u>cted; 10. <u>chin a</u>ctually; 11. sho<u>w a les</u>s; 12. <u>Russ, I a</u>lways;
13. <u>in dia</u>monds; 14. <u>Can a da</u>y; 15. <u>I ran</u>.

CHALLENGE #49

church; tomato; headache; eraser; sense; edited; onion; estates; stylist; legible.

CHALLENGE #50

1. send; 2. tender; 3. defend; 4. depend; 5. lender; 6. offend; 7. pretend;
8. amend; 9. friend; 10. calendar; 11. dividend; 12. mend; 13. endangered;
14. Nintendo; 15. trend.
Bonus Round: ascend; blend; apprehend.